icecreamtreats

easy ways to transform
your favorite ice cream into
spectacular desserts

icecreamtreats

charity ferreira

photographs by leigh beisch

CHRONICLE BOOKS

SAN FRANCISCO

For Damon

Some very generous people helped me with this book. Many thanks to Rebecca Allswang, Lisl Hampton, Kelly Evans Pfeifer, and Sara Sens for their meticulous and enthusiastic recipe testing. Thanks also to my tireless cadre of tasters: Michael and Chris Ferreira; Damon, Rebecca, and Jackie Allswang; Cliff Ingham; and Michael Goorjian. I am especially indebted to Kate Washington, for sharing her unique ability to be both precise and inspired, and above all to Debbie Hughes, for keeping the hot lines open no matter how often I call.

Text copyright © 2004 by Charity Ferreira.
Photographs copyright © 2004 by Leigh Beisch.

Library of Congress Cataloging-in-Publication Data available.

ISBN 0-8118-4102-2

Manufactured in China.

Designed and typeset by Benjamin Shaykin
Prop styling by Sara Slavin
Food styling by Amy Nathan and Elisabet derNederlanden
Photo Assistant: Angelica Arriaga
Typset in Gotham, Filosofia, Peregroy, and Neapolitan
Special thanks to Sue Fisher King for the generous use of some props.

Distributed in Canada by Raincoast Books
9050 Shaughnessy Street
Vancouver, British Columbia V6P 6E5

10 9 8 7 6 5 4 3 2

Chronicle Books LLC
85 Second Street
San Francisco, California 94105

www.chroniclebooks.com

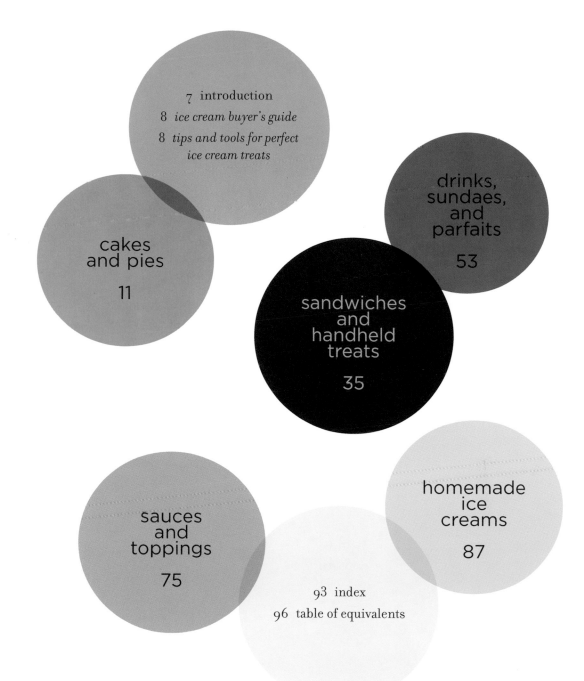

introduction

When it comes to desserts, I have always been an ice cream person, in the way that some people are cake people while others yearn for fresh fruit pie. I became keenly aware of this when I worked at Greens restaurant in San Francisco, where I had the opportunity to assist Debbie Hughes, a brilliant and talented pastry chef with a highly evolved philosophy of ice cream.

Surrounded by beautiful raw ingredients, and hopped-up on caffeine and sugar, I learned at Greens that desserts can feed much more than just a craving for something sweet. They can be whimsical, intellectual, and fun. It goes without saying that a great dessert tastes delicious, but it also satisfies on other levels, whether because it's beautiful, evokes a memory, or makes you smile in appreciation of its simplicity. And no desserts seem to do that as well as those involving ice cream.

The last several years have seen an amazing increase in both the variety and availability of high-quality store-bought ice cream. Although it's hard to improve on the simplicity of a bowl of good ice cream, just a few deft additions—a fruit topping, a crumb crust, a chewy gingersnap, or a layer of butter cake—turn purchased ice cream into special and evocative desserts.

The recipes in this book will show you how to use purchased ice cream to make cakes and pies, ice cream sandwiches, sundaes, layered parfaits, and drinks that range from homey to elegant, as well as homemade sauces and toppings to embellish them. Use your imagination to come up with your own creations. And if you want to try your hand at making your own ice cream, there are recipes for some classic flavors—dark chocolate, coffee bean, vanilla bean, and strawberry—as well.

ice cream buyer's guide

When buying ice cream at the supermarket, there are basically two kinds to choose between: premium and nonpremium. Although these denominations sound like they indicate quality, it's more accurate to say they indicate the *style* of the ice cream, and which you choose is a matter of personal preference.

Premium ice cream (brands like Häagen-Daz, Ben & Jerry's, and Dreyer's Dreamery) is most often sold by the pint, and is denser and richer than nonpremium ice cream. This is because it contains more solids and less air than nonpremium ice creams, such as Dreyer's Grand and store brands, which have a lighter, softer texture. If you eat a lot of ice cream, you're probably familiar with the differences between these two types. If in doubt, compare the nutrition labels and the prices. Premium ice cream is more expensive, and it contains nearly twice the calories and fat of nonpremium ice cream.

Because nonpremium ice cream has more air, it softens more evenly and is easier to spread. However, for the same reason, it also melts faster. This can lead to iciness in the finished dessert if the ice cream melts too much as you work.

Some of the recipes in this book call for "3 pints premium or ½ gallon nonpremium ice cream." This is because nonpremium ice cream tends to pack down more when you soften and spread it. In an ice cream cake, 3 pints of premium ice cream will look like about the same volume as a ½ gallon of nonpremium.

A few of these recipes specify one type or the other, but most call for either. If the recipe does not specify a particular type, either will work.

A final note on a third type of ice cream: I love Philadelphia-style ice cream (which is made without eggs), such as Breyers, for eating in sundaes and parfaits. But I avoid using this kind of ice cream for ice cream cakes and pies. It tends to melt very quickly, which makes it difficult to work with and can give the cake or pie an icy texture.

tips and tools for perfect ice cream treats

before you begin

Check to make sure you have adequate room in your freezer for what you plan to make. You don't want to assemble a beautiful ice cream dessert only to have it melt while you make space for it in the freezer.

Have your work space clear and your tools and ingredients on hand before taking the ice cream out of the freezer to minimize the time the ice cream spends at room temperature.

Try to work with ice cream in a cool kitchen rather than one warm from the mid-day heat or the oven.

use the right tools for the job

While this won't always mean the difference between success and failure, it often makes the difference between a seamless experience and a frustrating one. Keep in mind that sometimes the most efficient tool for the job is a pair of clean hands; don't be afraid to use them! Here are a few other implements that will make assembly go smoothly.

OFF-SET SPATULA   This tool has a narrow angled blade with a rounded tip, which makes it easy to spread and frost the outsides of cakes evenly. Off-set spatulas come in several sizes— 6 and 8 inches are good all-purpose lengths. Shorter ones are handy for finer detailed work, or for spreading ice cream between cookies for ice cream sandwiches.

For spreading ice cream into a pie crust or cake pan, I use a triangular spatula with an angled metal blade. I think the one I favor is actually a pie server, but its short, wide blade makes it easy to exert enough pressure to spread stiff ice cream smoothly.

FLEXIBLE HEATPROOF SPATULA   I use these spatulas for everything. They are indispensable for evenly scraping the bottom of a saucepan, and for folding dry ingredients into batter.

CHEF'S KNIFE   A large, heavy-duty knife is essential for cutting through frozen ice cream. A well-maintained chef's knife (my favorite is 8 inches) is as important for making desserts as it is for cooking savory foods; it is the best tool for chopping nuts and chocolate, and slicing ice cream cakes and pies.

PARCHMENT PAPER   Baking parchment is sold in rolls at many grocery stores and baking supply stores. It keeps cookies from sticking while baking, and you can re-use the same piece for several batches of cookies.

BOWLS   Use large bowls for mixing cake batters and cookie dough. A large bowl allows you to blend ingredients in fewer strokes without overworking the batter or dough, which is generally better for the texture of the finished product. I have a number of lightweight stainless-steel bowls in a variety of sizes, which work well for mixing or for melting chocolate over hot water.

PANS   I avoid dark-colored baking pans and baking sheets (including those with dark nonstick finishes); they hold heat in a way that causes the edges of cakes and the bottoms of cookies to become darkly browned. I prefer stainless-steel, aluminum, or other light-colored metal bakeware, which generally result in more even browning. Most of the ice cream cake recipes in this book call for a 9- or 10-inch springform cake pan. These pans have a removable outer rim that closes tightly around a round base. Aluminum springform pans are quite inexpensive at restaurant supply stores; be sure to get one with a rim at least 2½ inches tall.

FINE-MESH STRAINER   This is the one tool I could not do without. I use it to sift dry ingredients, to dust cocoa powder or powdered sugar on the tops of cakes or cookies, and to strain fruit sauces and custards.

ICE CREAM SCOOPS   Ice cream scoops come in a variety of sizes in kitchenware stores and restaurant supply stores, and they make a big difference in the presentation of ice cream. Larger ones are good for sundaes and ice cream sandwiches; smaller ones are nice for parfaits or bonbons. I prefer the kind with the mechanism on the handle that depresses to release perfectly rounded scoops.

SERVING DISHES Having a variety of attractive cake platters, footed sundae or parfait glasses, straws, and long-handled spoons is part of the fun of serving ice cream desserts.

softening tips

For sundaes, parfaits, and ice cream sandwiches, ice cream need only be soft enough to scoop easily. For making ice cream cakes and pies, however, you want your ice cream to be soft enough to spread, but not so soft that it melts as you work. The easiest way I have found to soften ice cream evenly is to microwave the carton on full power at 10-second intervals for up to about 40 seconds, stopping every 10 seconds to stir or break up the ice cream with a knife or spatula so that the outside doesn't melt before the center softens. You can also let the ice cream stand at room temperature for 10 to 15 minutes, stirring it occasionally to encourage even softening.

Keep in mind that nonpremium ice cream will soften more quickly than premium ice cream because it has more air, and that sorbet, because of its high sugar content, will soften even more quickly.

storing

One of the greatest advantages of many of the ice cream desserts in this book is that they can be assembled several days ahead of time. Each recipe has individual storage guidelines, but a few general principles apply:

Depending on how cold your freezer is, it is a good idea to turn it to the coldest setting. If your freezer affects your refrigerator's temperature, be sure to move delicate vegetables and other perishables to the warmest part of the refrigerator.

Before freezing, wrap ice cream treats well in plastic wrap when called for, to prevent ice crystals from forming.

slicing and serving

Let cakes and pies stand at room temperature for 5 to 10 minutes before slicing. It is easiest to cut ice cream cakes on a flat surface before transferring to a serving platter, because the metal cake pan bottoms can slide around on the platter as you slice. To cut cakes and pies neatly, dip the blade of a large, sharp knife in hot water and wipe it dry before cutting each slice.

cakes
and
pies

Strawberry Cheesecake Pie, page 17

I'm not the only one obsessed by ice cream cakes and pies. I am amazed at how many people have told me that such treats are traditional birthday desserts in their family. It makes perfect sense, of course, to have your ice cream and cake or pie happily married in one dessert, rather than serving a piece of cake with a lonely scoop of ice cream melting next to it.

There is an ice cream cake or pie here for everyone, and for every occasion. Tiramisù Ice Cream Cake (page 19) is a dressed-up vehicle for coffee ice cream. Black Bottom Chocolate Cream Pie (page 32) will satisfy the most ardent chocolate lover. Berry Pudding Cake (page 20), layers of berry sorbet and angel food cake, would make a beautiful, light dessert for a shower or a summer lunch. Frozen Cassata with Bittersweet Chocolate Glaze (page 14) is an elegant ending to a holiday meal or dinner party.

Not that you need a special occasion to enjoy these treats . . . an ice cream cake or pie is its own reason to celebrate. Try experimenting with different ice cream flavors to come up with your own favorite combinations.

black forest ice cream cake

MAKES 10 TO 12 SERVINGS Cherry–chocolate chip ice cream with a devil's food cake base and kirsch-spiked whipped cream is delicious with Hot Fudge Sauce (page 77).

to make devil's food cake: Preheat oven to 350°F. Butter and flour a 9-inch springform pan. In a bowl, with an electric mixer, beat butter and sugar until smooth and well blended. Beat in egg. In another bowl, stir together flour, cocoa, baking powder, and salt. Stir half the flour mixture into butter mixture. Stir in milk, followed by remaining flour mixture, and mix until well blended. Scrape batter into pan and smooth top. Bake until a skewer inserted into the center comes out clean, 25 to 30 minutes. Remove pan rim and cool cake completely on a wire rack.

Replace pan rim around cooled cake but do not close it tightly. Line inside of the rim with strips of parchment or waxed paper wide enough to come slightly above the top of the rim (about 3 inches wide); tighten rim around cake. Soften ice cream (see softening tips, page 10), and spread over cake in pan, smoothing the top. Place plastic wrap directly on surface of ice cream and freeze until firm, at least 8 hours and up to 2 days.

to make chocolate shavings: Drag a vegetable peeler firmly along block of chocolate, letting shavings fall onto a piece of parchment paper.

to make whipped cream: In a bowl, with a mixer on high speed, whip cream with sugar until it holds medium peaks. Beat in kirsch, if using. Take ice cream cake from freezer and remove plastic wrap, pan rim, and the parchment strip. Spread whipped cream over top and sides of cake. Sprinkle the top and sides of the cake with chocolate shavings. Return to freezer until whipped cream is firm, about 15 minutes or up to 1 day.

To serve, remove cake from freezer and let stand at room temperature 5 to 10 minutes. To slice cake neatly, dip the blade of a large, sharp knife in hot water and wipe it dry before cutting each slice. Serve immediately.

devil's food cake

6 tablespoons unsalted butter, softened*

3/4 cup sugar

1 egg

3/4 cup all-purpose flour

1/2 cup Dutch-processed cocoa powder

1 teaspoon baking powder

1/4 teaspoon salt

1/2 cup milk

3 pints premium or 1/2 gallon nonpremium cherry–chocolate chip ice cream or cherry ice cream

One 6- to 8-ounce piece semisweet chocolate, for chocolate shavings

1 1/4 cups heavy cream

2 tablespoons sugar

1 1/2 tablespoons kirsch (optional)

* *To soften butter, microwave it for a few seconds or place it near the preheating oven until soft but not melting.*

frozen cassata with bittersweet chocolate glaze

MAKES 10 TO 12 SERVINGS   This rich vanilla ice cream cake incorporates the flavors of Italian cannoli filling—ricotta, chocolate, pistachios, and orange peel. A standing mixer with a paddle attachment is the easiest way to incorporate the ingredients into the ice cream. If you don't have one, use a sturdy wooden spoon; a handheld electric mixer is not strong enough for the job. Be sure to let the glaze cool before pouring it on the cake; if it's warm it will melt the ice cream.

crust

2 cups amaretti cookie crumbs (10 ounces)

5 tablespoons unsalted butter, melted

3 tablespoons sugar

filling

15 ounces part-skim ricotta (not low-fat)

2 tablespoons sugar

1 teaspoon vanilla extract

½ gallon nonpremium vanilla ice cream

3 ounces bittersweet chocolate, finely chopped, or ½ cup miniature chocolate chips

½ cup pistachios, chopped

1 tablespoon minced orange zest

glaze

4 ounces bittersweet chocolate, chopped

⅓ cup cream

2 teaspoons light corn syrup

to make the crust: Preheat oven to 350°F. In a bowl, mix crumbs, butter, and sugar until well combined. Press mixture evenly into the bottom and about 1 inch up the sides of a 9-inch springform pan. Bake until crust is slightly toasted and feels dry to the touch, 12 to 15 minutes. Cool completely.

to make the filling: In a small bowl, mix ricotta, sugar, and vanilla until well blended. Soften ice cream (see softening tips, page 10). In the bowl of a standing mixer fitted with a paddle attachment, beat ice cream at low speed, just until creamy but not melted. Beat in ricotta mixture, chocolate, pistachios, and orange zest. Working quickly, spread ice cream into crust, smoothing top. Place a sheet of plastic wrap directly on the surface of the ice cream and freeze until firm, at least 8 hours or up to 2 days.

to make the glaze: Bring about 2 inches water to a boil in a saucepan or the bottom of a double boiler; remove from heat. Combine chocolate, cream, and corn syrup in a heatproof bowl or in the top of double boiler. Set bowl over hot water and let stand, stirring occasionally until melted and smooth, about 15 minutes. Let glaze cool to room temperature, until thickened but still fluid enough to spread easily, about 20 minutes.

Take cake from freezer and remove plastic wrap. Spread glaze evenly over the top, smoothing the surface with an off-set spatula. Return cake to freezer until glaze is set, about 20 minutes or up to 1 day.

To serve, remove cake from freezer and let stand 5 to 10 minutes. Run a knife along inside rim of pan to loosen cake. Remove pan rim. To slice cake, dip the blade of a large knife in hot water and wipe dry between each slice. Serve immediately.

boston ice cream pie

MAKES 10 TO 12 SERVINGS In this frozen version of the classic custard-filled dessert, a delicate sponge cake is topped with French vanilla ice cream and a shiny bittersweet chocolate glaze.

sponge cake

3 large eggs

7 tablespoons sugar

¾ cup cake flour

1 teaspoon baking powder

⅛ teaspoon salt

½ teaspoon vanilla extract

½ gallon nonpremium French vanilla ice cream

glaze

4 ounces bittersweet chocolate, chopped

⅓ cup cream

2 teaspoons light corn syrup

to make sponge cake: Preheat oven to 350°F. Butter and flour a 9-inch springform pan. In large bowl, with a mixer on high speed, beat eggs and sugar until very thick and pale yellow, 5 to 8 minutes. In a small bowl, stir together cake flour, baking powder, and salt; sift over the egg mixture. Gently fold in flour mixture just until incorporated. Gently fold in vanilla. Pour batter into pan and spread it out to the edges. Bake until top of cake springs back when lightly pressed in the center, 18 to 20 minutes. Remove pan rim and cool cake on a wire rack.

Replace pan rim around cake but do not close. Line inside of pan rim with strips of parchment or waxed paper wide enough to come above top of rim (about 3 inches wide); tighten rim around cake. Soften ice cream (see softening tips, page 10), and spread over cake, smoothing the top. Place plastic wrap directly on surface of ice cream. Freeze until firm, at least 8 hours and up to 2 days.

to make glaze: Bring about 2 inches water to a boil in a saucepan or the bottom of a double boiler; remove from heat. Combine chocolate, cream, and corn syrup in a heatproof bowl or in the top of double boiler. Set bowl over hot water and let stand, stirring occasionally, until melted and smooth, about 15 minutes. Let glaze cool until thickened but still fluid enough to spread easily, about 20 minutes.

Take cake from freezer and remove plastic wrap. Spread room-temperature glaze evenly over the top, smoothing surface. Return cake to freezer until glaze is set, about 20 minutes or up to 1 day.

To serve, remove cake from freezer and let stand 5 to 10 minutes. Remove plastic wrap, pan rim, and parchment paper. To slice cake, dip the blade of a large knife in hot water and wipe it dry between each slice. Serve immediately.

strawberry cheesecake pie

MAKES 8 TO 10 SERVINGS This cheesecake pie is covered with a tangy sour cream topping. If you prefer, you can instead glaze it with strawberry jam or Fresh Strawberry Topping (see Note). Serve wedges of the pie with Berry Sauce (page 80) made with strawberries and sliced fresh strawberries.

to make crust: Preheat the oven to 350°F. In a large bowl, mix crumbs, butter, and sugar until well combined. Press into the bottom and up sides of a 9-inch pie pan. Bake until crust is lightly toasted and feels dry to the touch, 12 to 15 minutes. Cool completely.

Soften ice cream (see softening tips, page 10). Carefully spread ice cream into crust, smoothing the top. Place a sheet of plastic wrap directly on the surface of pie and freeze until firm, at least 8 hours or up to 2 days.

to make sour cream topping: In a bowl, with an electric mixer on high speed, beat cream, sour cream, sugar, and vanilla together until mixture holds soft peaks. Remove pie from freezer and remove plastic wrap. Spread topping over ice cream, smoothing the top. Freeze until topping is firm, about 20 minutes or up to 1 day.

To serve, remove pie from freezer and let stand at room temperature 5 to 10 minutes. To slice pie neatly, dip the blade of a large, sharp knife in hot water and wipe it dry before cutting each slice. Serve Immediately.

note

If you prefer a strawberry glaze to a sour cream topping, spread 1/2 cup room-temperature strawberry jam or Fresh Strawberry Topping (page 81) evenly over ice cream. Freeze until glaze is firm, about 20 minutes or up to 1 day.

crust

1½ cups graham cracker crumbs (about 6 ounces)

5 tablespoons unsalted butter, melted

2 tablespoons sugar

2 pints premium or 1½ quarts nonpremium strawberry cheesecake ice cream

sour cream topping

¾ cup heavy cream

½ cup sour cream

2 tablespoons sugar

1 teaspoon vanilla extract

tiramisù ice cream cake

MAKES 10 TO 12 SERVINGS Once you have lined the pan with ladyfingers, which is admittedly a little painstaking, this impressive-looking dessert couldn't be easier to assemble. Packaged ladyfingers generally come in two varieties: the softer kind, which is like sponge cake, and the hard, crunchy ones. Use the latter for this recipe.

Line the sides of a 9-inch springform pan with ladyfingers by standing them up vertically, edge to edge, along the inside rim of the pan. Line the bottom of the pan completely with remaining ladyfingers, trimming cookies as needed to completely cover the bottom of the pan in an even layer. Using a pastry brush, brush the exposed sides of ladyfingers generously with rum.

Soften ice cream (see softening tips, page 10). Spread evenly in pan, smoothing the top. Place a sheet of plastic wrap directly on the surface of the ice cream and freeze until firm, at least 8 hours or up to 2 days.

In a bowl, with a mixer on medium speed, beat mascarpone with sugar and vanilla until smooth. Slowly beat in cream until incorporated (stopping to scrape the sides of the bowl as necessary), then beat at high speed until soft peaks form. Remove cake from freezer and take off plastic wrap. Spread mascarpone cream over ice cream layer, smoothing the top. Freeze until cream is firm, about 20 minutes or up to 1 day.

To serve, remove cake from freezer and let stand at room temperature 5 to 10 minutes. Remove pan rim. Dust top of cake with cocoa powder. To slice cake neatly, dip the blade of a large, sharp knife in hot water and wipe it dry before cutting each slice. Serve immediately.

30 to 35 crunchy ladyfingers (about 10 ounces)

½ cup dark rum

3 pints premium or ½ gallon nonpremium coffee ice cream

4 ounces mascarpone cheese

2 tablespoons sugar

2 teaspoons vanilla extract

1 cup heavy cream

Unsweetened cocoa powder, for dusting

berry pudding cake

MAKES 6 TO 8 SERVINGS Somewhere between a trifle and a summer pudding, these layers of angel food cake, berry sorbet, and whipped cream make a light and beautiful summer dessert. Resist the temptation to spend a long time frosting the cake with whipped cream, or the sorbet will begin to melt. Garnish the top with fresh berries, if you like.

About twelve ¾-inch-thick slices angel food cake (purchased or homemade)

2 pints raspberry, blackberry, or strawberry sorbet

1¼ cups heavy cream

1½ tablespoons sugar

½ teaspoon vanilla extract

Line a rectangular 8½-by-4½-inch loaf pan (1½–quart capacity) with two sheets of plastic wrap, leaving several inches of overhang on all sides. Line the bottom of pan completely with a single layer of angel food cake slices, cutting cake slices as needed to fit.

Soften sorbet (see softening tips, page 10). Spread 1 pint of the sorbet over cake in pan bottom. Top with another even layer of cake slices and spread the second pint of sorbet over cake layer. Top with a final layer of cake slices, pressing down top to compress the layers. Wrap tightly with overhanging plastic wrap and freeze until firm, at least 8 hours and up to 2 days.

In a large bowl, with an electric mixer on high speed, whip cream with sugar and vanilla until it holds medium peaks. Unwrap cake, invert loaf pan onto a serving plate, and lift off pan. Remove plastic wrap from cake. Working quickly, frost top and sides of cake generously with whipped cream. Freeze until cream is firm, about 20 minutes or up to 1 day.

To serve, with sharp knife, cut cake crosswise into 1-inch-thick slices, wiping the blade clean between cutting each slice. Serve immediately.

eggnog ice cream torte

with rum whipped cream

MAKES 10 TO 12 SERVINGS   This is a festive, easy Christmas dessert, perfect with Caramel Sauce (page 78) and a cup of spiced cider or mulled wine.

crust

2 cups finely ground gingersnap cookie crumbs, from Gingersnaps (page 45) or purchased gingersnap cookies (about 8 ounces)

6 tablespoons unsalted butter, melted

3 tablespoons sugar

½ gallon nonpremium eggnog ice cream

rum whipped cream

1 cup heavy cream

1 tablespoon sugar

1 tablespoon rum

Ground or freshly grated nutmeg for garnish

to make crust: Preheat oven to 350°F. In a bowl, mix crumbs, butter, and sugar until well combined. Press into the bottom and about 1 inch up sides of a 9-inch springform pan. Bake until crust is lightly toasted and feels dry to the touch, 12 to 15 minutes. Cool completely.

Soften ice cream (see softening tips, page 10), and gently spread into crust in pan, smoothing the top. Place a sheet of plastic wrap directly on surface of ice cream and freeze until firm, at least 8 hours and up to 2 days.

to make whipped cream: In a bowl, with an electric mixer on high speed, whip cream with sugar and rum until cream holds soft peaks. Take cake from freezer and remove plastic wrap. Spread whipped cream over top of cake and sprinkle with nutmeg. Freeze until cream is firm, about 20 minutes or up to 1 day.

To serve, remove cake from freezer and let stand at room temperature 5 to 10 minutes. Run a knife along the inside rim of pan to loosen cake. Remove pan rim. To slice cake neatly, dip the blade of a large, sharp knife in hot water and wipe it dry before cutting each slice. Serve immediately.

butter pecan pie

Butter pecan is typically a seasonal flavor, available in winter. For a delicious summer alternative, try this vanilla wafer crust and butterscotch topping with a good-quality peach ice cream.

to make crust: Preheat oven to 350°F. In a large bowl, mix crumbs, butter, and sugar until well combined. Press into the bottom and up sides of a 9-inch pie pan. Bake until crust is lightly toasted and feels dry to the touch, 10 to 12 minutes. Cool completely.

Soften ice cream (see softening tips, page 10). Gently spread into crust, smoothing the top. Place a sheet of plastic wrap directly on the surface of ice cream and freeze until firm, at least 8 hours or up to 2 days.

Remove pie from freezer and take off plastic wrap. Use a spoon to drizzle a decorative lattice pattern of butterscotch sauce over the top of pie. Freeze pie until butterscotch is firm, about 20 minutes or up to 1 day.

To serve, remove pie from freezer and let stand at room temperature 5 to 10 minutes. To slice pie neatly, dip the blade of a large, sharp knife in hot water and wipe it dry before cutting each slice. Serve immediately.

crust

- 1½ cups vanilla wafer cookie crumbs (about 6 ounces)
- 5 tablespoons unsalted butter, melted
- 2 tablespoons sugar
- ½ gallon butter pecan ice cream
- ½ cup Butterscotch Sauce (page 80) or purchased butterscotch sauce, at room temperature

german chocolate ice cream pie

MAKES 10 TO 12 SERVINGS This ice cream pie is topped with a fluffy mountain of caramel whipped cream, toasted coconut, and pecans. Häagen-Daz makes a German chocolate cake ice cream flavor, which is an appropriate and delicious alternative to the chocolate ice cream.

Preheat oven to 350°F. Toast pecans on a baking sheet until golden, about 10 minutes. Cool and coarsely chop. Toast coconut, stirring it several times until it is evenly browned, 5 to 8 minutes. Leave oven on.

to make crust: In a large bowl, mix crumbs, butter, and sugar until well combined. Press evenly into the bottom and up sides of a 9-inch pie pan. Bake until crust is lightly toasted around the edges and feels dry to the touch, 10 to 12 minutes. Cool completely.

Soften ice cream (see softening tips, page 10). Carefully spread ice cream into crust, smoothing the top. Place a piece of plastic wrap directly on the surface of the ice cream and freeze until firm, at least 8 hours or up to 2 days.

Spoon caramel sauce into a large bowl. In another bowl, with a mixer on high speed, whip cream until it holds medium peaks. Stir about one third of the whipped cream into the caramel sauce. With a flexible spatula, gently fold in the remaining whipped cream.

Remove pie from freezer and take off plastic wrap. Whisk the cream gently to thicken to a spreadable consistency, if necessary, and spread over the ice cream, mounding the cream slightly in the center. Sprinkle with coconut and pecans. Freeze pie until whipped cream is firm, about 30 minutes or up to 1 day.

To serve, remove pie from freezer and let stand at room temperature 5 to 10 minutes. To slice pie neatly, dip the blade of a large, sharp knife in hot water and wipe it dry before cutting each slice. Serve immediately.

¾ cup pecan pieces

¾ cup sweetened flaked coconut

crust

1½ cups chocolate cookie crumbs (about 6 ounces)

5 tablespoons unsalted butter, melted

2 tablespoons sugar

2 pints premium or 1½ quarts nonpremium chocolate ice cream or German chocolate cake ice cream

½ cup Caramel Sauce (page 78) or purchased caramel sauce, at room temperature

1 cup heavy cream

mochimbouche

SERVES 8 TO 10   Sushi is a holiday tradition in my family; for virtually every birthday, we bring cake and presents to the same family-owned Japanese restaurant and settle in for an evening of sushi and sake. For my husband's birthday one year, I made a towering pyramid of ice cream–filled mochi, my Japanese take on *croquembouche,* the elaborate French dessert made of cream puffs stuck together with caramel.

Mochi ice cream balls are covered with a delicious chewy rice coating. They come in a variety of flavors and are available at Asian markets, many grocery stores, and Trader Joe's. Make the pyramid with your favorite flavor, or use a combination, such as vanilla and mango, or chocolate and green tea. Buy them a day or two before you plan to make the mochimbouche so they are firmly frozen before you assemble this dessert.

You'll need a 10-inch round cardboard cake circle, available at cake- or candy-making supply stores (or you might prevail on a friendly bakery to give you one) to assemble this dessert.

24 mochi ice cream balls, any flavor (or a combination)

8 ounces white chocolate, finely chopped

¼ cup colored candy sprinkles (optional)

Remove mochi from packages and place on a baking sheet. Dust the cornstarch coating off each piece with a dry pastry brush to ensure that the white chocolate will stick to the surface. Place baking sheet in freezer.

Bring about 2 inches water to a boil in a saucepan or the bottom of a double boiler; remove from heat. Place chocolate in a heatproof bowl or in the top of double boiler. Set bowl over hot water and let stand, stirring frequently until melted and smooth, 10 to 15 minutes.

Place cardboard circle on a flat work surface. To make the first layer, remove 12 mochi balls from the freezer. Place 3 balls in a flat triangle shape in the center of the circle, with sides touching. Spoon white chocolate between the balls at the points where they connect, and gently press them together (don't worry about being neat; the whole pyramid

(continued)

gets drizzled with melted chocolate at the end). Surround the 3 balls with 9 more balls, so that you have a single-layer, filled-in circle of mochi balls. Once the balls are positioned, spoon white chocolate at all points where balls touch.

To make the second layer, remove 7 more mochi balls from the freezer. Dip the bottom of 1 ball in chocolate and center it on top of your original triangle. Surround with 6 more balls, dipping the bottom of each in chocolate, so that you have a second, smaller circle sitting on top of the first. Spoon chocolate at all points where balls touch.

To make the third layer, remove 4 mochi balls from the freezer. Dip the bottoms of the balls in chocolate and center the 4 balls in a square on top of the second layer. Spoon chocolate at points where balls touch.

Remove last mochi ball from the freezer. Dip the bottom in chocolate, and center it on top of the third layer. Drizzle remaining chocolate over the pyramid and decorate with sprinkles, if desired. Freeze at least 1 hour. When chocolate is set, the dessert can be covered loosely with plastic wrap and frozen up to 1 day.

To serve, remove from freezer and place cardboard circle on a serving plate. Tap chocolate with a knife to break mochi balls apart; place individual balls on plates and serve immediately.

cookie dough ice cream cake

MAKES 10 TO 12 SERVINGS This buttery blondie looks like a giant chocolate chip cookie after it's baked. The blondie is halved like a layer cake and filled with cookie dough ice cream. Serve wedges of the cake with Hot Fudge Sauce (page 77) on the side to push this cookie-lover's dessert over the top.

to make chocolate chip blondie: Preheat oven to 325°F. Butter and flour a 10-inch springform pan. In a bowl, with an electric mixer, beat butter, brown sugar, and granulated sugar until blended and smooth. Beat in eggs and vanilla until well blended, scraping down sides of bowl as necessary. In another bowl, stir together flour, baking powder, baking soda, and salt. Stir half the flour mixture into butter mixture. Stir in milk, followed by remaining flour mixture, just until well blended. Stir in chocolate chips. Spread batter evenly into pan and bake until a skewer inserted into the center comes out clean, 45 to 50 minutes. Remove pan rim and cool cake completely on a wire rack.

Halve blondie horizontally with a serrated knife. Remove top layer, leaving bottom half of the cake on the pan base. Replace pan rim around cake but do not close it tightly. Line the inside of the pan rim with strips of parchment or waxed paper wide enough to come slightly above the top of rim (about 3 inches wide); tighten rim around cake.

Soften ice cream (see softening tips, page 10), and spread on bottom layer, smoothing the top. Place top layer of blondie over ice cream, compressing slightly. Cover with plastic wrap and freeze until firm, at least 8 hours and up to 2 days.

To serve, remove ice cream cake from freezer and remove plastic wrap, pan rim, and parchment strip. Let cake stand at room temperature 5 to 10 minutes. To slice cake neatly, dip the blade of a large, sharp knife in hot water and wipe it dry before cutting each slice. Serve immediately.

chocolate chip blondie

3/4 cup (1½ sticks) unsalted butter, softened*

3/4 cup firmly packed dark brown sugar

3/4 cup granulated sugar

3 eggs

1 teaspoon vanilla extract

2 cups all-purpose flour

1 teaspoon baking powder

½ teaspoon baking soda

½ teaspoon salt

¼ cup milk

1 cup chocolate chips

3 pints premium or ½ gallon nonpremium cookie dough ice cream

* To soften butter, microwave it for a few seconds or place it near the preheating oven until soft but not melting.

frozen lemon meringue pie

MAKES 8 TO 10 SERVINGS This refreshing sorbet pie with a warm, gooey meringue top is great with Berry Sauce (page 80). Because the pie is baked to brown the meringue prior to serving, it is especially important that the pie be frozen solid before baking.

crust

1½ cups graham cracker crumbs (about 6 ounces)

5 tablespoons unsalted butter, melted

2 tablespoons sugar

2 pints lemon sorbet

meringue topping

2 egg whites

¼ cup sugar

to make crust: Preheat oven to 350°F. In a large bowl, mix crumbs, butter, and sugar until well combined. Press into the bottom and up sides of a 9-inch pie pan. Bake until crust is lightly toasted around the edges and feels dry to the touch, 12 to 15 minutes. Cool completely.

Soften sorbet (see softening tips, page 10). Gently spread into crust, smoothing the top. Place a sheet of plastic wrap directly on the surface of sorbet and freeze until firm, at least 12 hours or up to 2 days.

to make meringue topping: In a bowl set over a pan of barely simmering water, stir egg whites and sugar with a flexible spatula until sugar is dissolved and mixture is slightly warm. Remove bowl from heat. Beat with a mixer on high speed until mixture holds stiff, shiny, moist-looking peaks.

Remove pie from freezer and take off plastic wrap. Spread meringue on top of pie, spreading it out to the edges to cover all of the sorbet. Freeze until meringue is firm, at least 1 hour or up to 1 day.

At least 10 minutes before baking, preheat oven to 500°F. Bake pie on middle rack just until meringue is lightly browned, 4 to 5 minutes. Serve immediately.

black bottom chocolate cream pie

MAKES 8 TO 10 SERVINGS If you love chocolate, this triple-chocolate pie is for you: chocolate ice cream in a chocolate cookie crust, topped with a cloud of chocolate whipped cream. Go for chocolate four ways and garnish the pie with chocolate shavings, if you like.

crust

1½ cups chocolate cookie crumbs (about 7 ounces)

5 tablespoons unsalted butter, melted

2 tablespoons sugar

2 pints premium or 1½ quarts nonpremium chocolate ice cream

4- to 6-ounce piece semisweet chocolate, for chocolate shavings (optional)

1 cup heavy cream

3 tablespoons Dutch-process cocoa powder

3 tablespoons powdered sugar

to make crust: Preheat the oven to 350°F. In a large bowl, mix crumbs, butter, and sugar until well combined. Press into the bottom and sides of a 9-inch pie pan. Bake until crust is lightly toasted and feels dry to the touch, 12 to 15 minutes. Cool completely.

Soften ice cream (see softening tips, page 10). Gently spread into crust, smoothing the top. Place a sheet of plastic wrap directly on the surface of ice cream and freeze until firm, at least 8 hours or up to 2 days.

to make chocolate shavings: Drag a vegetable peeler firmly along block of chocolate, letting chocolate shavings fall onto a piece of waxed or parchment paper.

In a bowl, with an electric mixer on high speed, whip cream until slightly thickened. Sift cocoa powder and powdered sugar over cream and whip gently until it holds soft peaks.

Remove pie from freezer and take off plastic wrap. Spread chocolate whipped cream over top of ice cream, mounding the cream slightly in the center. Sprinkle chocolate shavings over top of pie, if desired. Freeze until whipped cream is firm, about 20 minutes or up to 1 day.

To serve, remove pie from freezer and let stand at room temperature 5 to 10 minutes. To slice neatly, dip the blade of a large, sharp knife in hot water and wipe it dry before cutting each slice. Serve immediately.

tin roof sundae pie

MAKES 8 TO 10 SERVINGS What do you get when you cross a s'more and a baked Alaska? This pie, with its combination of chocolate-and-marshmallow ice cream, a crust made of peanut butter sandwich cookies, and a warm fluffy meringue topping. Because the pie is baked to brown the meringue, it is especially important that the pie be frozen solid before baking.

to make crust: Preheat the oven to 350°F. In a large bowl, mix crumbs, butter, and sugar until well combined. Press into the bottom and up sides of a 9-inch pie pan. Bake until crust is lightly toasted around the edges and feels dry to the touch, 12 to 15 minutes. Cool completely.

Soften ice cream (see softening tips, page 10). Gently spread into crust, smoothing the top. Place a sheet of plastic wrap directly on surface of ice cream and freeze until firm, at least 8 hours or up to 2 days.

to make meringue topping: In a bowl set over a pan of barely simmering water, stir egg whites and sugar with a flexible spatula until sugar is dissolved and mixture is slightly warm. Remove bowl from heat. Beat with a mixer on high speed until mixture holds stiff, shiny, moist-looking peaks.

Remove pie from freezer and take off plastic wrap. Spread meringue on top of pie, spreading it out to the edges to cover all of the ice cream. Freeze until meringue is firm, at least 1 hour or up to 1 day.

At least 10 minutes before baking, preheat oven to 500°F. Bake pie on middle rack just until meringue is lightly browned, 4 to 5 minutes. Serve immediately.

crust

1½ cups finely ground peanut butter sandwich cookie crumbs, such as Nutterbutters (about 7 ounces)

3 tablespoons unsalted butter, melted

2 tablespoons sugar

2 pints premium or 1½ quarts non-premium rocky road, heavenly hash, or tin roof sundae ice cream

meringue topping

2 egg whites

¼ cup sugar

coconut ice cream cake

MAKES 10 TO 12 SERVINGS Coconut layer cake, that ethereal combination of butter cake, whipped cream, and flaked coconut, never fails to please. In this version, coconut ice cream replaces of most of the cake, which only improves matters.

coconut butter cake

5 tablespoons unsalted butter, softened*

½ cup sugar

1 egg

1 egg yolk

1 teaspoon vanilla extract

1 cup cake flour

1 teaspoon baking powder

⅛ teaspoon salt

½ cup milk

½ cup sweetened flaked coconut

3 pints premium coconut ice cream

1¼ cups heavy cream

2 tablespoons sugar

1 teaspoon vanilla extract

¼ teaspoon coconut extract (optional)

2 cups sweetened flaked coconut

To soften butter, microwave it for a few seconds or place it near the preheating oven until soft but not melting.

to make coconut butter cake: Preheat oven to 350°F. Butter and flour a 9-inch springform pan. In a bowl, with a mixer on medium-high speed (use paddle attachment if using standing mixer), beat butter and sugar until fluffy and pale yellow, 2 to 3 minutes. Gradually beat in egg, egg yolk, and vanilla, beating well after each addition and scraping down the sides of the bowl as necessary, until well blended.

In another bowl, combine flour, baking powder, and salt. Sift half the flour mixture over butter mixture and stir or beat at low speed just until incorporated. Stir in milk. Sift remaining flour mixture over batter and stir in, followed by coconut. Scrape batter into prepared pan and smooth top. Bake until a skewer inserted in the center comes out clean, 20 to 25 minutes. Remove pan rim and cool cake on a wire rack.

Replace pan rim around cake but do not close it tightly. Line inside of pan rim with strips of parchment or waxed paper wide enough to come above the top of rim (about 3 inches wide); tighten rim. Soften ice cream (see softening tips, page 10), and spread in pan, smoothing top. Place plastic wrap directly on the surface of ice cream and freeze until firm, at least 8 hours and up to 2 days.

In a bowl, with a mixer on high speed, whip cream with sugar, vanilla, and coconut extract (if using), until it holds medium peaks. Take cake from freezer and remove plastic wrap, pan rim, and the parchment strips. Spread whipped cream over top and sides of cake. Sprinkle flaked coconut over the top and press into the sides of the cake. Return the cake to freezer until whipped cream is firm, about 20 minutes or up to 1 day.

To serve, remove cake from freezer and let stand at room temperature 5 to 10 minutes. To slice cake, dip the blade of a large knife in hot water and wipe it dry before cutting each slice. Serve immediately.

sandwiches and handheld treats

Coffee-Toffee Sandwiches
with Oatmeal Cookies, page 37

Ice cream sandwiches are one of the most cheerful and satisfying desserts I know. They can be made ahead, and they're just the right size for dessert or a snack. They can be as elegant as raspberry sorbet between cacao nib meringues (page 49), or as casual as fudgey walnut brownies spread with pistachio ice cream (page 38).

An assortment of ice cream sandwiches, such as the dulce de leche ice cream with Mexican wedding cookies (page 41), the strawberry ice cream with chocolate snaps (page 44), and the mint-chip cookies with mint-chip ice cream (page 42), would make a fun dessert for a child's birthday party. Rum-soaked babas filled with vanilla ice cream (page 46) will make you glad to be an adult.

Use these combinations as a starting point for your own inventions—the possibilities are limitless. And if you don't have time to bake your own cookies, there are plenty of good-quality packaged or bakery cookies to choose from.

coffee-toffee sandwiches
with oatmeal cookies

MAKES ABOUT 12 SANDWICHES Use parchment paper to keep these crisp oatmeal cookies from sticking to the pans when you bake them. The unadorned cookies make superb ice cream sandwiches, but I recommend taking the extra step of glazing the cookies with dark chocolate before assembling the sandwiches.

to make oatmeal cookies: In a bowl, with a mixer on medium-high speed (use paddle attachment if using standing mixer), beat butter and brown sugar together until well blended. Beat in egg and vanilla, scraping down sides of bowl as necessary. In a small bowl, stir together flour, oats, baking soda, and salt; stir or beat into butter mixture. Stir in almonds. Cover and refrigerate dough until thoroughly chilled, at least several hours or overnight.

Preheat oven to 350°F. With lightly floured hands, roll dough into 1-inch balls and place 2 to 3 inches apart on parchment paper–lined baking sheets. Bake until cookies are spread out and well browned, 12 to 15 minutes. Cool completely before removing from baking sheets.

to make chocolate glaze: Bring about 2 inches water to a boil in a saucepan or the bottom of a double boiler; remove from heat. Combine chocolate and butter in a heatproof bowl or in the top of double boiler. Set bowl over hot water and let stand, stirring occasionally with a flexible spatula, until melted and smooth, about 15 minutes.

Place cookies in a single layer on baking sheets. Using a knife, spread chocolate glaze on tops of cookies. Chill until set, about 15 minutes, or let stand at room temperature until completely set, about 1½ hours.

To assemble, soften ice cream slightly. Place a large scoop of ice cream (about ⅓ cup) on flat (bottom) side of 1 cookie; top with another cookie, bottom-side down. Press gently to compress the ice cream and bring it out to the edges of the cookies. Repeat process to fill remaining cookies with ice cream. Serve the sandwiches immediately, or wrap individually in plastic wrap and freeze for up to 1 week.

oatmeal cookies

- ½ cup (1 stick) unsalted butter, softened*
- 1 cup firmly packed dark brown sugar
- 1 egg
- ½ teaspoon vanilla extract
- 1 cup all-purpose flour
- ¾ cup regular rolled oats
- ½ teaspoon baking soda
- ⅛ teaspoon salt
- ½ cup toasted almonds, chopped

chocolate glaze

- 8 ounces bittersweet chocolate, finely chopped
- 2 tablespoons unsalted butter

- 2 pints premium coffee-toffee ice cream, such as Ben & Jerry's Coffee Heath Bar Crunch

* To soften butter, microwave it for a few seconds or place it near the preheating oven until soft but not melting.

pistachio sandwiches with walnut brownies

MAKES 12 SANDWICHES These thin, chewy brownies make a classic ice cream sandwich paired with just about any flavor of ice cream. My favorite is a dense layer of premium pistachio, but feel free to substitute your flavor of choice.

walnut brownies

6 tablespoons unsalted butter, cut in ½-inch pieces

5 ounces unsweetened chocolate, chopped

3 eggs

1½ cups sugar

1 teaspoon vanilla extract

¾ cup all-purpose flour

½ teaspoon baking powder

¼ teaspoon salt

1 cup walnut pieces

2 pints premium or 1½ quarts nonpremium pistachio ice cream

to make walnut brownies: Butter a 12-by-15-inch jelly-roll pan. Line bottom of pan with a parchment paper rectangle cut to fit; butter parchment. Lightly dust pan with flour.

Preheat oven to 350°F. Bring about 2 inches water to a boil in a saucepan or the bottom of a double boiler; remove from heat. Combine butter and chocolate in a heatproof bowl or in the top of double boiler. Set bowl over hot water and let stand, stirring occasionally until melted and smooth, about 15 minutes.

In another bowl, whisk eggs, sugar, and vanilla together. Stir chocolate into egg mixture until blended. In another bowl, combine flour, baking powder, and salt. Stir flour mixture until blended.

Spread batter evenly in pan and sprinkle with walnuts. Bake until edges feel firm and a skewer inserted into the center comes out with moist crumbs attached, 18 to 20 minutes. Cool completely in pan.

Run a knife along inside edge of pan to release brownie. Place a piece of aluminum foil on a flat surface. Invert pan over foil to release brownie. Trim about ¼ inch from the edges, and then cut brownie in half lengthwise down the center to make two rectangles, each about 12 by 7 inches.

Soften ice cream (see softening tips, page 10). Gently spread the ice cream evenly over one of the brownie halves. Place the other brownie half, walnut-side up, on ice cream; gently compress to flatten the sandwich and bring the ice cream out to the edges. Wrap the foil securely around the brownie and freeze until firm, at least 8 hours or up to 2 days.

Remove brownie from freezer and remove foil. Using a sharp knife, cut into 12 rectangles. Serve sandwiches immediately, or wrap individually in plastic wrap and freeze up to 2 days.

dulce de leche sandwiches

with mexican wedding cookies

MAKES 12 SANDWICHES These cookies are a slightly sweeter, richer version of the traditional Mexican wedding cookie. Rolling and freezing the dough in a long cylinder makes it easy to slice and bake into uniformly round cookies that are perfect for ice cream sandwiches. It also means that you can keep the dough in the freezer for up to 3 weeks and bake the cookies when needed for an impromptu dessert.

to make cookies: In a bowl, with a mixer on medium speed (use paddle attachment if using standing mixer), beat 1½ cups powdered sugar and butter together until smooth. Beat in egg and vanilla until well incorporated, scraping down sides of bowl as necessary. In a small bowl, stir together flour, baking powder, and salt; stir or beat into butter mixture. Stir in pecans. Spoon dough in a row lengthwise along a piece of plastic wrap and, with lightly floured hands, shape into a cylindrical log that is about 9 inches long and about 2½ inches wide. Roll in the plastic wrap and freeze until firm enough to slice, at least several hours or overnight.

Preheat oven to 325°F. Remove dough from freezer and cut crosswise into slices about ¼ inch thick. Place about 1 inch apart on buttered or parchment paper–lined baking sheets. Bake until dry to the touch and slightly brown on the edges, 18 to 22 minutes. Sprinkle tops of cookies generously with powdered sugar and transfer to a wire rack to cool completely.

To assemble, soften ice cream slightly (see softening tips, page 10). Place a large scoop of ice cream (about ⅓ cup) on flat (bottom) side of 1 cookie; top with another cookie, bottom-side down. Press gently to compress the ice cream and bring it out to the edges of the cookies. Repeat process to fill remaining cookies with ice cream. Serve the sandwiches immediately, or wrap individually in plastic wrap and freeze for up to 1 week.

mexican wedding cookies

- 1½ cups powdered sugar, plus additional for sprinkling
- 1 cup (2 sticks) unsalted butter, softened*
- 1 egg
- 1 teaspoon vanilla extract
- 2 cups all-purpose flour
- ¾ teaspoon baking powder
- ¼ teaspoon salt
- 1 cup toasted pecans, finely chopped
- 2 pints premium or 1½ quarts nonpremium *dulce de leche* ice cream

* To soften butter, microwave it for a few seconds or place it near the preheating oven until soft but not melting.

grasshopper sandwiches

MAKES ABOUT 12 SANDWICHES These mint-chip cookie sandwiches are cute when made with bright green mint-chip ice cream, and slightly classier made with white mint-chip ice cream. If you can't decide which to use, make some of each.

mint-chip cookies

1 cup (2 sticks) unsalted butter, softened*

1¼ cups powdered sugar

½ teaspoon peppermint extract

½ teaspoon vanilla extract

1 egg

2 cups all-purpose flour

½ teaspoon baking powder

¼ teaspoon salt

⅔ cup miniature chocolate chips

1½ quarts mint-chip ice cream

To soften butter, microwave it for a few seconds or place it near the preheating oven until soft but not melting.

to make mint-chip cookies: Preheat oven to 350°F. In a bowl, with an electric mixer on medium-high speed (use paddle attachment if using standing mixer), beat butter, powdered sugar, peppermint extract, and vanilla until smooth. Beat in egg, scraping down sides of bowl as necessary. In a small bowl, mix flour, baking powder, and salt; stir or beat into butter mixture. Stir in chocolate chips.

With lightly floured hands, shape dough into balls slightly larger than 1 inch in diameter; flatten each ball between your palms into a round about 2½ inches wide. Place 1 inch apart on parchment paper–lined baking sheets. (If the dough is too sticky to work with, refrigerate it for about 15 minutes or until it is firm enough to handle.) Bake until cookies feel firm to touch and are just beginning to turn golden on the edges, 12 to 15 minutes. Cool completely.

To assemble, soften ice cream slightly (see softening tips, page 10). Place a large scoop of ice cream (about ⅓ cup) on flat (bottom) side of 1 cookie; top with another cookie, bottom-side down. Press gently to compress the ice cream and bring it out to the edges of the cookies. Repeat process to fill remaining cookies with ice cream. Serve the sandwiches immediately, or wrap individually in plastic wrap and freeze for up to 1 week.

strawberry sandwiches

with chocolate snaps

MAKES ABOUT 15 SANDWICHES   This chocolate snap is a variation on a recipe for chewy ice cream sandwich cookies from pastry chef and food writer Carolyn Weil. The cookie dough will hold for several days in the refrigerator. Roll the sides of these sandwiches in chocolate or colored candy sprinkles for a fun children's birthday party dessert.

chocolate snaps

6 ounces bittersweet chocolate, finely chopped

½ cup (1 stick) unsalted butter, cut in chunks

⅓ cup sugar

¼ cup light corn syrup

1 egg

1⅓ cup all-purpose flour

½ teaspoon baking soda

½ teaspoon baking powder

¼ teaspoon salt

2 pints premium or 1½ quarts nonpremium strawberry ice cream

About 2 cups candy sprinkles

to make chocolate snaps: In a large heatproof bowl set over a pan of barely simmering water, stir chocolate, butter, sugar, and corn syrup together until melted and smooth. Remove from heat and let cool about 5 minutes; whisk in egg. In another bowl, combine flour, baking soda, baking powder, and salt; stir into chocolate mixture until blended. Cover and refrigerate until dough is thoroughly chilled and firm, at least several hours or overnight.

Preheat oven to 350°F. With lightly floured hands, roll generous tablespoons of dough into 1-inch balls. Place balls 2 to 3 inches apart on parchment paper–lined cookie sheets. Bake until edges are firm and the tops are dry and set, 13 to 15 minutes. Allow cookies to cool 5 minutes on baking sheets, then transfer to wire racks to cool completely.

To assemble, soften ice cream slightly (see softening tips, page 10). Place a large scoop of ice cream (about ⅓ cup) on flat (bottom) side of 1 cookie; top with another cookie, bottom-side down. Press gently to compress the ice cream and bring it out to the edges of the cookies. Repeat process to fill remaining cookies with ice cream. Roll the sides of the sandwiches in sprinkles spread in a shallow bowl. Serve immediately or wrap sandwiches individually in plastic and freeze for up to 3 days.

pumpkin sandwiches with gingersnaps

MAKES ABOUT 12 SANDWICHES   When the weather begins to turn crisp, scoops of seasonal pumpkin ice cream between sumptuous, crackly gingersnaps make a welcome dessert or snack. When pumpkin ice cream is not available, try peach or strawberry ice cream.

to make gingersnaps: Preheat oven to 375°F. In a bowl, with a mixer on medium-high speed (use paddle attachment if using standing mixer), beat butter, brown sugar, and granulated sugar until smooth. Beat in egg and molasses until well blended, scraping down sides of bowl as necessary. In a small bowl, stir together flour, baking soda, baking powder, salt, ginger, cinnamon, and cloves; stir or beat into butter mixture. Cover and refrigerate dough until firm enough to handle, about 1 hour.

With lightly floured hands, roll dough into 1¼-inch balls. In a shallow dish, roll balls in turbinado sugar to coat and place about 2 inches apart on parchment paper–lined baking sheets. Bake until edges are firm to the touch and tops have a crackled appearance, 13 to 15 minutes. Allow cookies to cool 5 minutes on baking sheets, then transfer to wire racks to cool completely.

To assemble, soften ice cream slightly (see softening tips, page 10). Place a large scoop of ice cream (about ⅓ cup) on flat (bottom) side of 1 cookie; top with another cookie, bottom-side down. Press gently to compress the ice cream and bring it out to the edges of the cookies. Repeat process to fill remaining cookies with ice cream. Serve the sandwiches immediately, or wrap individually in plastic wrap and freeze for up to 1 week.

gingersnaps

¾ cup plus 2 table-spoons (1¾ sticks) unsalted butter, softened*

¾ cup firmly packed dark brown sugar

½ cup granulated sugar

1 egg

¼ cup dark molasses

2½ cups all-purpose flour

1½ teaspoons baking soda

½ teaspoon baking powder

¼ teaspoon salt

1 tablespoon ground ginger

1 teaspoon ground cinnamon

⅛ teaspoon ground cloves

Turbinado or other large-crystal sugar, for coating

2 pints premium or 1½ quarts nonpre-mium pumpkin ice cream

* To soften butter, microwave it for a few seconds or place it near the preheating oven until soft but not melting.

ice cream babas

MAKES 6 BABAS What could be better than tender, rum-soaked brioche filled with cream? Rum babas filled with ice cream, of course. Try them with Vanilla Bean Ice Cream (page 89). You can let this dough rise in the refrigerator overnight; if you do, let the dough stand at room temperature for about 2 hours before shaping the babas and placing them in ramekins.

You can make the rum syrup up to a day ahead. Store it in the refrigerator and reheat it gently before dipping the babas. Plan to soak the babas in syrup about 30 minutes before you're going to serve them.

babas

1 teaspoon active dry yeast

¼ cup warm (110°F) water

¼ cup milk

1 egg, lightly beaten

1½ tablespoons sugar

1½ cups to 1¾ cups all-purpose flour

½ teaspoon salt

3 tablespoons unsalted butter, softened*

rum syrup

¾ cup water

¾ cup sugar

¼ cup rum

1 quart vanilla ice cream

* To soften butter, microwave it for a few seconds or place it near the preheating oven until soft but not melting.

to make babas: In the bowl of a standing mixer, dissolve yeast in the warm water. Let stand until foamy, about 10 minutes. Stir in milk, egg, and sugar. With the paddle attachment, beat in 1½ cups of the flour and salt (dough will be very soft and sticky). Beat 1 to 2 minutes at medium speed until well blended, then beat in butter a few chunks at a time until well incorporated. Continue to mix at medium speed (lower the speed if mixer starts to labor) 4 to 5 minutes longer, adding up to ¼ cup more flour if necessary to make the dough pull from the sides of the bowl. Scrape dough down if it crawls up beater; also scrape bowl sides as necessary to incorporate all ingredients. Remove the beater and scrape it clean.

Scrape dough onto a well-floured board and knead a few times to bring together. Return to bowl, cover with plastic wrap, and let stand in a warm place until doubled, 1½ to 2 hours. Press gently to expel air.

Lightly butter six 4-ounce-capacity ramekins. Turn dough out onto a floured surface and divide into 6 equal pieces. Roll each piece into a ball. Place each ball in a ramekin, cover ramekins loosely with plastic wrap, and let rise until puffy and nearly doubled, about 45 minutes. Meanwhile, preheat oven to 375°F.

Place ramekins directly on the middle rack of the oven and bake until well browned on top, 18 to 20 minutes. Remove babas from ramekins and cool completely.

to make rum syrup: In a small saucepan over medium heat, stir water and sugar together until sugar is dissolved. Bring the mixture to a boil and remove from heat. Stir in rum.

At least 30 minutes but no more than an hour before serving, slice babas in half horizontally. Dip halves one at a time into warm syrup, turning to saturate all sides and allowing each to soak in the syrup for about 30 seconds. Place halves on a wire rack until completely cool.

To serve, place bottom half of baba on a plate and top with a large scoop of ice cream. Cover with top half of baba. Serve immediately.

raspberry sorbet sandwiches
with cocoa nib meringues

MAKES ABOUT 12 SANDWICHES Serve these elegant, nearly fat-free sandwiches on plates drizzled with Chocolate Syrup (page 77). Alternatively, fill the sandwiches with chocolate sorbet and serve with Berry Sauce made with raspberries (page 80). For best results, bake the meringues on baking sheets lined with parchment paper.

to make the meringues: Preheat oven to 250°F. Using a wine glass as a guide, draw 12 evenly spaced, 2½-inch-diameter circles on each of 2 sheets parchment paper. Line 2 baking sheets with the parchment, ink-side down.

In a large bowl, with a mixer on high speed, beat egg whites with cream of tartar until thick and foamy. Add granulated sugar in a slow, steady stream and continue to beat until the mixture holds stiff, shiny peaks. Sift powdered sugar over and gently fold in. Fold in cacao nibs.

Drop a heaping tablespoon meringue mixture in the center of each circle outlined on the parchment and, with the back of a spoon, gently spread each meringue out to the circle edges in a flat, even layer.

Bake meringues until dry and firm to touch on the outside and almost dry inside, 40 to 50 minutes. Switch position of baking sheets midway through baking time so that meringues spend an equal amount of time on the top and bottom rack of the oven. Cool completely on baking sheets. The meringues can be stored in an airtight container for up to 2 days.

To assemble, soften sorbet (see softening tips, page 10). Place a large scoop (about ⅓ cup) on the flat side of a meringue. Gently spread the ice cream out to the edges of the meringue with a knife; gently top with a second meringue, bottom-side down. Repeat process to assemble remaining sandwiches. Dust tops of meringues with cocoa powder. Serve immediately, or wrap sandwiches individually and freeze up to 3 days.

cacao nib meringues

3 large egg whites, at room temperature

¼ teaspoon cream of tartar

½ cup granulated sugar

½ cup powdered sugar

2 tablespoons finely chopped cacao nibs or bittersweet chocolate*

2 pints raspberry or chocolate sorbet

Unsweetened cocoa powder, for garnish

* Cacao nibs are unsweetened bits of roasted cocoa bean that taste exactly like what they are—the very essence of chocolate. Look for them at specialty food stores, or order them online from Scharffen Berger Chocolate Maker (www.scharffenberger.com).

bonbons

MAKES ABOUT 24 BONBONS These chocolate-dipped ice cream balls have many guises. I like to sprinkle them with cocoa powder and serve them in paper truffle cups with after-dinner coffee. But it's also nice to have a batch in the freezer to enjoy with popcorn while you're watching a movie.

When scooping and dipping these ice cream balls, the most important thing is to keep them as cold as possible; if they start melting they will lose their shape and be difficult to dip.

I experimented with a truffle fork, a dinner fork, and a wooden skewer before realizing that the easiest and most efficient way to dip the ice cream balls in the melted chocolate was to use my fingers.

2 pints premium ice cream, any flavor (preferably without chunks)

1 pound bittersweet chocolate, finely chopped

3 tablespoons solid vegetable shortening

Freeze a baking sheet for about 20 minutes.

Soften 1 pint of the ice cream slightly (see softening tips, page 10; work with 1 pint at a time to avoid melting the second pint), just until soft enough to scoop. Remove baking sheet from the freezer and line it with parchment or waxed paper.

Use a small 1-inch ice cream scoop (available at kitchen-supply stores) to scoop the ice cream into compact balls on baking sheet. Repeat with second pint (move the sheet pan into the freezer as you work if the ice cream balls begin to melt). Wrap pan tightly in plastic wrap to prevent ice crystals from forming. Freeze until ice cream is very hard, at least 8 hours or overnight.

Line a second baking sheet with parchment or waxed paper and place in the freezer to chill while you melt the chocolate. (This sheet will hold the bonbons after they have been dipped in chocolate.)

Bring about 2 inches water to a boil in a saucepan or the bottom of a double boiler; remove from heat. Combine chocolate and shortening in a heatproof bowl or in the top of double boiler. Set bowl over hot water

(continued)

BONBONS *continued*

and let stand, stirring occasionally with a flexible spatula, until melted and smooth, about 15 minutes. Remove bowl from over hot water and let stand until lukewarm but still fluid, 15 to 20 minutes.

Remove both baking sheets from freezer and unwrap the ice cream balls. Working quickly, drop 1 ice cream ball at a time into the chocolate mixture. Roll it quickly in the chocolate to coat, and then lift it out, cradling the bottom of the bonbon with your fingertips. Shake it gently to let excess chocolate drip off and place on the second baking sheet. If the undipped ice cream balls start to melt as they're waiting to be dipped, return the pan to the freezer and remove 1 ball at a time as you continue to dip them.

Place the sheet of dipped bonbons in the freezer for about 1 hour. Transfer to an airtight container with a piece of waxed paper between each layer and freeze up to 1 week.

drinks, sundaes, and parfaits

Butterscotch Milk Shake, page 59

These are the simplest of all ice cream treats, requiring only that you layer, pile, or blend ice creams, sauces, and toppings to create desserts that are even more delicious than their individual components.

In this chapter, you'll find a variety of milk shakes and ice cream sodas that go far beyond the classics, ice cream parfaits that showcase seasonal fresh fruit, and the ultimate ice cream sundae guide.

Whether you're making an impromptu shake or float, a layered parfait, or a gooey sundae, be sure to serve it with a long-handled spoon for getting the last of the ice cream from the bottom of the glass.

chocolate malted milk shake

MAKES 1 TO 2 SERVINGS   This thick, chocolatey shake is the old-fashioned malted of your childhood memories. Try making it with Dark Chocolate Ice Cream (page 91) and sprinkle chopped chocolate-covered malt balls over the top.

Combine all ingredients in a blender container and blend until smooth. Pour into tall, chilled glasses and serve immediately with straws.

- 1 pint chocolate ice cream
- ½ cup milk
- ¼ cup malted milk powder
- 2 tablespoons Chocolate Syrup (page 77) or purchased chocolate syrup

variations

VANILLA MALTED   Substitute vanilla ice cream for the chocolate; omit chocolate syrup.

COFFEE MALTED   Substitute coffee ice cream for the chocolate; omit chocolate syrup.

CARAMEL MALTED   Substitute vanilla ice cream for the chocolate and Caramel Sauce (page 78) or purchased caramel sauce for the chocolate syrup.

berry-vanilla milk shake

MAKES 1 TO 2 SERVINGS This pretty shake reminds me of the soft ice cream sometimes called "smoosh-ins," in which fruit and other ingredients are worked into soft vanilla ice cream on a marble slab. Try making this shake with Vanilla Bean Ice Cream (page 89).

In a blender container, blend 1 cup of the ice cream with the berries and milk until smooth. With a spoon, stir in remaining ice cream, leaving white streaks remaining. Pour into tall chilled glasses and serve immediately with straws and long-handled spoons.

1 pint vanilla ice cream, softened

1 cup fresh or frozen raspberries, black-berries, strawberries, or blueberries

½ cup milk

espresso milk shake

MAKES 1 TO 2 SERVINGS My brother and I lived on these strong, coffee-fortified milk shakes in college. For the best coffee flavor, make this with strongly flavored ice cream such as the Coffee Bean Ice Cream on page 92. For a fully caffeinated experience, garnish the shakes with chocolate bark made with espresso beans (see page 85).

1 pint coffee ice cream

¼ cup milk

¼ cup cold espresso or very strong coffee

Combine all ingredients in a blender container and blend until smooth. Pour into tall chilled glasses and serve immediately with straws.

butterscotch milk shake

MAKES 1 TO 2 SERVINGS These creamy shakes are the perfect dessert for a casual summer barbecue.

Combine all ingredients in a blender container and blend until smooth. Pour into tall chilled glasses and serve immediately with straws.

1 pint vanilla ice cream

½ cup milk

¼ cup Butterscotch Sauce (page 80) or purchased butterscotch sauce

sherbet freeze

MAKES 1 TO 2 SERVINGS This blended shake is light and refreshing. If you have some on hand, add 2 tablespoons Berry Sauce (page 80) to the blender ingredients.

In a blender container, blend sherbet and club soda until smooth. Pour into tall chilled glasses and serve immediately with straws.

1 pint raspberry, orange, or pineapple sherbet

½ cup club soda or seltzer water

mocha frappé

MAKES 1 SERVING If you don't have access to freshly made espresso, dissolve 2 tablespoons instant espresso powder in ¼ cup boiling water; let cool before using.

1 cup coffee ice cream

1 cup crushed ice

¼ cup cold espresso

3 tablespoons Chocolate Syrup (page 77) or purchased chocolate syrup

Combine all ingredients in a blender container and blend until smooth. Pour into a tall chilled glass and serve immediately with a straw.

variation

COFFEE-CARAMEL FRAPPÉ Substitute Caramel Sauce (page 78) or purchased caramel sauce for the chocolate syrup.

chocolate cream soda

MAKES 1 SERVING For an intense chocolate flavor, try this fizzy classic with homemade Dark Chocolate Ice Cream (page 91). Leave room in the glass for the soda to bubble up once the ice cream is added.

Pour chocolate syrup into a tall glass. Add cream soda, followed by 1 to 2 scoops (about ½ cup) chocolate ice cream, depending on glass size. Top with a dollop of whipped cream, if desired, and serve immediately with a straw and a spoon.

2 tablespoons Chocolate Syrup (page 77) or purchased chocolate syrup

1 cup cream soda

1 to 2 scoops chocolate ice cream

About ¼ cup whipped cream (optional)

cherry-chocolate parfait

MAKES 2 SERVINGS Use a purchased plain chocolate cake, a cake made from a mix, or the Devil's Food Cake on page 13 for this recipe.

1 cup 1-inch cubes chocolate cake

1 pint vanilla ice cream

½ cup Chocolate Syrup (page 77) or Hot Fudge Sauce (page 77)

½ cup Fresh Cherry Topping (page 81) or bottled preserved cherries

Whipped cream or Chocolate Whipped Cream (page 86) for topping

In each of two tall parfait glasses, layer about ¼ cup of the cake cubes, ½ cup ice cream, 2 tablespoons chocolate syrup, and 2 tablespoons cherry topping. Repeat to make a second layer in each glass. Top each with whipped cream. Serve immediately.

peach crisp parfait

MAKES 2 SERVINGS This fresh, creamy parfait is a deconstructed peach crisp à la mode. Assemble it while the peaches are warm, so the ice cream melts into the cooked fruit.

1 tablespoon unsalted butter

¼ cup firmly packed dark brown sugar

¾ pound ripe peaches (about 2 small peaches) or nectarines, pitted and sliced ¼ inch thick

1 pint vanilla ice cream or vanilla frozen yogurt

1 cup crumbled Oatmeal Cookies (page 37) or purchased oatmeal cookies

In a nonstick frying pan, stir butter and brown sugar together over medium heat until melted and bubbly. Add peaches and cook, stirring frequently, until peaches are tender and juices have thickened slightly, about 5 minutes.

Working quickly, divide about half the peach mixture between two tall parfait glasses. Top the peaches in each glass with about ½ cup ice cream, followed by about ¼ cup crumbled cookies. Repeat layers in each glass, ending with cookies. Serve immediately.

strawberry-gingersnap parfait

MAKES 2 SERVINGS Strawberries and gingersnaps make a fresh, pretty parfait. Caramel ice cream is a delicious substitute for vanilla.

1 cup crumbled Gingersnap Cookies (page 45) or purchased gingersnap cookies

1 pint vanilla ice cream

½ cup Fresh Strawberry Topping (page 81)

1 cup sliced ripe strawberries

In each of two tall parfait glasses, layer about ¼ cup crumbled cookies, ½ cup ice cream, 2 tablespoons strawberry topping, and ¼ cup strawberries. Repeat layers in each glass, ending with strawberry layer. Serve immediately.

coconut tapioca parfait

MAKES 2 SERVINGS I am a huge fan of chewy tapioca desserts, and I love them even more when they involve ice cream. Tapioca pearls are available in various sizes in Asian markets. Their cooking time will vary depending on their size, so taste some to make sure they're cooked all the way through before removing from heat. This parfait is delicious made with warm tapioca, but if you prefer you can let the tapioca cool to room temperature before assembling the parfaits. The tapioca will set up firmly if chilled.

In a small saucepan over medium heat, stir water, coconut milk, and sugar together until dissolved. Add tapioca and simmer, stirring occasionally, until pearls are translucent and soft in the center, 10 to 15 minutes. Let tapioca cool about 15 minutes.

Spoon about one quarter of the tapioca mixture into the bottom of each of two parfait glasses. Top each with ½ cup mango sorbet. Repeat layers, ending with sorbet. Garnish the tops with flaked coconut, if desired. Serve immediately.

1 cup water

¾ cup coconut milk

¼ cup sugar

¼ cup tapioca pearls

1 pint mango sorbet or ice cream

Sweetened flaked coconut (optional)

butterscotch–banana pudding parfait

MAKES 2 SERVINGS Banana pudding aficionados will love what butterscotch sauce and custard-like French vanilla ice cream do for this gooey classic.

1 cup crumbled vanilla wafers (about 3 ounces), or 1 cup cubed Sponge Cake (page 16) or purchased sponge cake

2 cups French vanilla ice cream

2 small ripe bananas (about ½ pound total), peeled and sliced

½ cup Butterscotch Sauce (page 80) or purchased butterscotch sauce

In each of two tall parfait glasses, layer about ¼ cup crumbled cookies, ½ cup ice cream, one quarter of the sliced bananas, and 2 tablespoons butterscotch sauce. Repeat layers in each glass, ending with butterscotch sauce. Serve immediately.

the ultimate ice cream sundae

Happily, there is no wrong way to build an ice cream sundae. You can mix and match an unlimited variety of ice cream flavors, sauces, and toppings to create your own unique dessert. Use the components suggested here for inspiration, or try one of the following suggested combinations.

To host a party with a sundae bar, set up a selection of different ice creams, sauces, and toppings, set out sundae dishes, napkins, and spoons, and let everyone assemble their own.

ice creams

Vanilla Bean Ice Cream (page 89)
Strawberry Ice Cream (page 90)
Dark Chocolate Ice Cream (page 91)
Coffee Bean Ice Cream (page 92)
mint-chip ice cream
dulce de leche ice cream
toasted almond ice cream
berry sorbet
chocolate chip cookie dough ice cream
green tea ice cream
mango ice cream

sauces

Chocolate Syrup (page 77)
Hot Fudge Sauce (page 77)
Caramel Sauce (page 78)
Berry Sauce (page 80)
Dulce de Leche Sauce (page 79)
Butterscotch Sauce (page 80)

fruit toppings

Fresh Strawberry Topping (page 81)
Fresh Cherry Topping (page 81)
Brown Sugar–Pineapple topping (page 82)
sliced bananas
fresh berries
sliced peaches or nectarines

crunchy toppings

Toffee Almonds (page 83)
Chocolate Peanut Bark (page 85)
crumbled cookies
granola or other cereal
candy sprinkles
chopped malted milk balls
seasonal candies, such as peppermints
  or candy corns
chopped toasted nuts
sweetened flaked coconut
caramel corn or Cracker Jack
banana chips

fluffy toppings

Chocolate Whipped Cream (page 86)
Caramel Whipped Cream (page 86)
marshmallow creme
whipped cream

sundae combinations

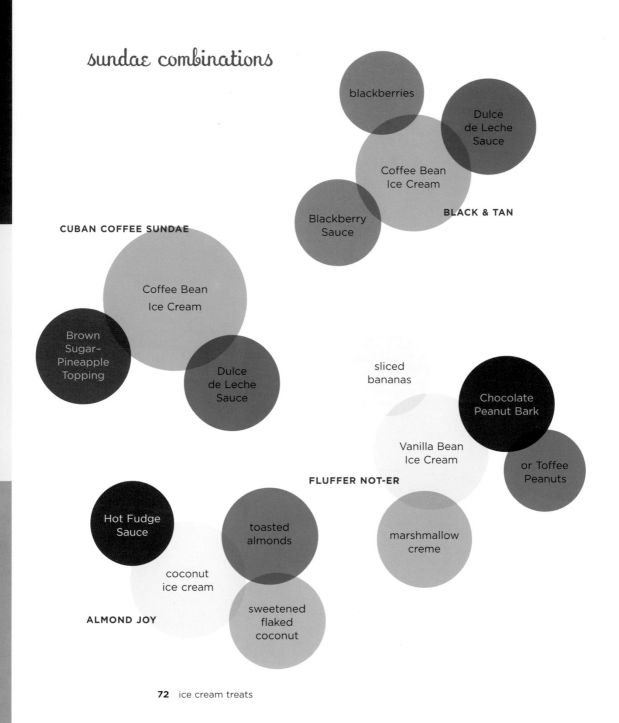

blackberries

Dulce de Leche Sauce

Coffee Bean Ice Cream

BLACK & TAN

CUBAN COFFEE SUNDAE

Blackberry Sauce

Coffee Bean Ice Cream

Brown Sugar–Pineapple Topping

Dulce de Leche Sauce

sliced bananas

Chocolate Peanut Bark

Vanilla Bean Ice Cream

or Toffee Peanuts

FLUFFER NOT-ER

Hot Fudge Sauce

toasted almonds

marshmallow creme

coconut ice cream

ALMOND JOY

sweetened flaked coconut

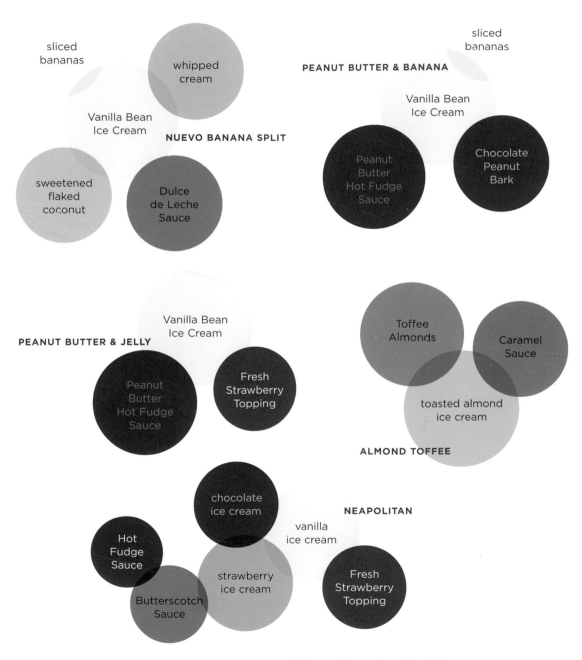

sliced
bananas

whipped
cream

Vanilla Bean
Ice Cream

NUEVO BANANA SPLIT

sweetened
flaked
coconut

Dulce
de Leche
Sauce

sliced
bananas

PEANUT BUTTER & BANANA

Vanilla Bean
Ice Cream

Peanut
Butter
Hot Fudge
Sauce

Chocolate
Peanut
Bark

Vanilla Bean
Ice Cream

PEANUT BUTTER & JELLY

Peanut
Butter
Hot Fudge
Sauce

Fresh
Strawberry
Topping

Toffee
Almonds

Caramel
Sauce

toasted almond
ice cream

ALMOND TOFFEE

chocolate
ice cream

NEAPOLITAN

vanilla
ice cream

Hot
Fudge
Sauce

Fresh
Strawberry
Topping

strawberry
ice cream

Butterscotch
Sauce

sundae combinations

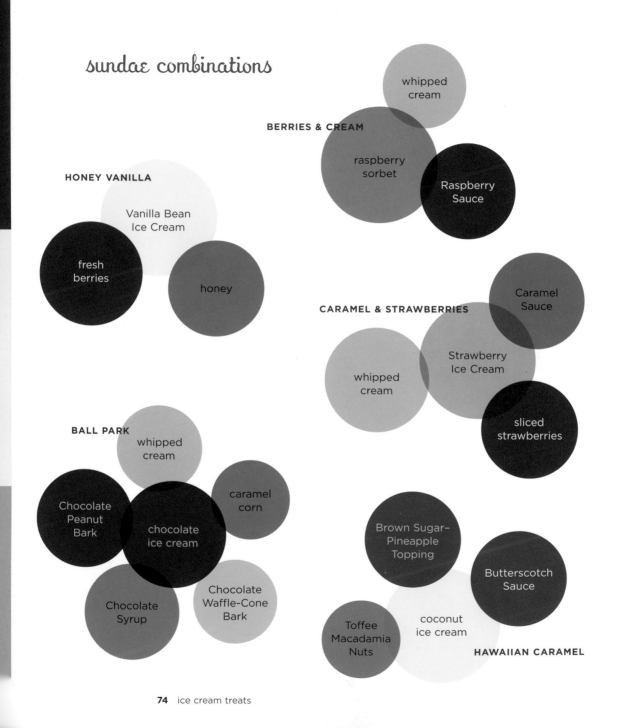

HONEY VANILLA

Vanilla Bean Ice Cream

fresh berries

honey

BERRIES & CREAM

whipped cream

raspberry sorbet

Raspberry Sauce

CARAMEL & STRAWBERRIES

Caramel Sauce

whipped cream

Strawberry Ice Cream

sliced strawberries

BALL PARK

whipped cream

caramel corn

Chocolate Peanut Bark

chocolate ice cream

Chocolate Syrup

Chocolate Waffle-Cone Bark

Brown Sugar–Pineapple Topping

Butterscotch Sauce

Toffee Macadamia Nuts

coconut ice cream

HAWAIIAN CARAMEL

sauces
and
toppings

When it comes to ice cream, a few simple accessories can make all the difference. A handful of toffee almonds or a spoonful of fruit topping or creamy caramel sauce is often all it takes to transform ice cream from something you eat out of the carton while standing in front of the freezer into a special dinner-party dessert. Most of these sauces and toppings can be made ahead and will keep for several weeks. These sauces also make great gifts, especially when paired with an ice cream scoop or a set of ice cream bowls or sundae glasses.

chocolate syrup

MAKES ABOUT 1½ CUPS This glossy chocolate syrup is liquid at room temperature, which makes it easy to add to ice cream sodas and floats.

2 tablespoons Dutch-process cocoa powder

2 tablespoons sugar

¾ cup water

1 tablespoon light corn syrup

5 ounces bittersweet chocolate, finely chopped

¼ teaspoon vanilla extract

In a small bowl, stir together cocoa powder and sugar. Bring water and corn syrup to a boil in a medium saucepan. Remove from heat and whisk in cocoa powder mixture, chocolate, and vanilla; continue whisking until smooth.

Tightly covered, the syrup will keep in the refrigerator for about 2 weeks.

hot fudge sauce

MAKES ABOUT 1¾ CUPS This hot fudge sauce is the real thing: dark, thick, and rich. Two ounces of unsweetened chocolate give it an intensely chocolatey edge, but it's also good made with all bittersweet chocolate.

Combine chocolates, corn syrup, brown sugar, cream, butter, and salt in a heatproof bowl or in the top of a double boiler. Bring 2 inches water to boil in a saucepan or bottom of double boiler. Remove pan from heat, place bowl with chocolate mixture over hot water, and let stand, stirring occasionally with a flexible spatula, until mixture is melted and smooth, about 15 minutes. Stir in vanilla.

Tightly covered, the sauce will keep about 2 weeks in the refrigerator. Warm it in the microwave or in a bowl set over a pan of hot water before serving.

6 ounces bittersweet chocolate, finely chopped

2 ounces unsweetened chocolate, finely chopped

½ cup light corn syrup

¼ cup firmly packed dark brown sugar

¼ cup heavy cream

¼ cup unsalted butter, cut in chunks

⅛ teaspoon salt

2 teaspoons vanilla extract

variation

PEANUT BUTTER HOT FUDGE SAUCE Melt 3 tablespoons smooth natural peanut butter with the other ingredients.

caramel sauce

MAKES 1½ CUPS A good caramel sauce is the perfect thing to have on hand for dressing up ice cream.

2 cups sugar

½ cup water

1 cup heavy cream

½ teaspoon vanilla extract

In a small heavy-bottomed saucepan, stir sugar and water together over medium heat until sugar is completely dissolved. Stop stirring, increase heat to high, and bring mixture to a boil. Boil mixture, without stirring, washing down the sides of the pan occasionally with a clean pastry brush dipped in water. As the sugar cooks, warm the cream for about 45 seconds in the microwave or in a saucepan over low heat.

Whenever the sugar mixture starts to caramelize around the edges of the pan, very carefully lift the pan and swirl the mixture gently to ensure even caramelization. Boil until sugar is a deep amber color, 5 to 10 minutes. Remove from heat and slowly pour warm cream into caramel (mixture will bubble up). Stir to blend. If caramel hardens on bottom or edges of pan, place over low heat and stir gently until dissolved. Stir in vanilla.

Tightly covered, the sauce will keep about 2 weeks in the refrigerator. Warm it slightly in the microwave or in a bowl set over a pan of hot water before serving.

dulce de leche sauce

MAKES ABOUT 1¾ CUPS If you remember the flavor of Milk-Maid caramels, you're close to imagining the flavor of this golden, unbelievably creamy caramel sauce. A long, gentle reduction over low heat give it its rich flavor and silky texture.

In a medium heavy-bottomed pot over medium heat, stir sugar into milk until sugar is dissolved and mixture comes to a boil. Stir in baking soda (the milk will become very foamy) and reduce heat to maintain a low simmer. Cook, stirring the bottom of the pot occasionally with a flexible heatproof spatula to prevent scorching, until mixture is a deep golden brown and reduced to 1¾ cups, 1 to 1½ hours.

Serve warm or at room temperature. Tightly covered, the sauce will keep about 2 weeks in the refrigerator.

1¼ cups sugar

4 cups whole milk

½ teaspoon baking soda

butterscotch sauce

MAKES 1¼ CUPS   This tastes just like old-fashioned ice-cream-parlor butterscotch. Use it on an ice cream sundae, in a Butterscotch Milk Shake (page 59), or just spoon it over a big bowl of vanilla ice cream.

1½ cups firmly packed dark brown sugar

¼ cup (½ stick) unsalted butter

2 tablespoons light corn syrup

½ teaspoon fresh lemon juice

2 tablespoons vanilla extract

½ cup heavy cream

In a medium heavy-bottomed saucepan over low heat, stir together brown sugar, butter, corn syrup, and lemon juice until melted and smooth. Increase heat to medium and cook for 2 to 3 minutes, stirring occasionally, until bubbling and foamy. Carefully stir in vanilla (mixture may splatter) and cook another minute. Stir in cream and remove from heat.

Serve warm or at room temperature. The sauce can be covered and refrigerated for about 2 weeks.

berry sauce

MAKES ABOUT 1½ CUPS   Use this recipe to make a bright, sweet-tart raspberry, strawberry, or blackberry sauce that is wonderful over vanilla ice cream or frozen yogurt.

1 pound fresh or thawed frozen raspberries, hulled strawberries, or blackberries

½ teaspoon fresh lemon juice

4 to 6 tablespoons sugar

In a blender or food processor, purée berries until smooth. Strain purée through a fine-mesh strainer into a bowl, pressing with a flexible spatula to extract as much juice as possible from the seeds and pulp. Whisk in lemon juice and sugar to taste. Sauce can be covered and refrigerated for up to 1 week.

fresh strawberry topping

MAKES 2 CUPS   This syrupy fresh jam is the quintessential banana-split topping, and it's not bad on a peanut butter sandwich, either.

In a medium saucepan, combine strawberries and sugar. Stir over low heat until sugar is dissolved and strawberries have released their juices, about 8 minutes. Lower heat and simmer, uncovered, stirring occasionally, until strawberries have broken down and mixture has thickened to a loose, jam-like consistency, about 30 minutes. Stir in lemon juice.

Serve the topping chilled or at room temperature. Tightly covered, it will keep several weeks in the refrigerator.

1½ pounds fresh straw-
   berries, rinsed, hulled,
   and sliced

1 cup sugar

1 tablespoon fresh
   lemon juice

fresh cherry topping

MAKES 2 CUPS   Ripe cherries cooked in sugar and their own juices are delicious over ice cream or in parfaits. A tablespoon of brandy is a nice addition to these fresh preserves.

In a medium saucepan, combine cherries and sugar. Stir over low heat until sugar is dissolved and cherries have released their juices, about 10 minutes. Lower heat and simmer, uncovered, stirring occasionally, until cherries are soft and mixture has thickened slightly, about 40 minutes.

Stir in lemon juice and almond extract. Serve the topping warm, chilled, or at room temperature. Tightly covered, it will keep several weeks in the refrigerator.

1½ pounds fresh cher-
   ries, rinsed, pitted,
   and halved

1 cup sugar

1 tablespoon fresh
   lemon juice

¼ teaspoon almond
   extract

brown sugar–pineapple topping

MAKES 1 CUP Even if a fresh pineapple seems spiny and unyielding, it's worth the effort of cutting into one to make this sweet-tart topping with a caramelized sugar flavor. Spoon it over vanilla ice cream and sprinkle with toffee macadamia nuts for a Hawaiian-style sundae.

2½ cups ½-inch chunks peeled and cored fresh pineapple (about half of a 3½-pound pineapple)

¾ cup firmly packed light brown sugar

In a large pot, combine pineapple and brown sugar. Stir frequently over medium heat until sugar is dissolved and juices are bubbling, 3 to 5 minutes. Lower heat and simmer, uncovered, stirring occasionally, until fruit has broken down and mixture has thickened slightly, about 30 minutes. Serve the topping warm, chilled, or at room temperature. Tightly covered, it will keep several weeks in the refrigerator.

toffee almonds

MAKES ABOUT 4 CUPS   A bag of these crunchy nuts and a jar of Hot Fudge Sauce (page 77) would make a great gift for an ice cream lover. Sprinkle the nuts on ice cream sundaes, or finely chop them to cover the sides of ice cream sandwiches or cakes.

In a medium pot over medium heat, stir together sugar, corn syrup, water, butter, and salt until melted and bubbling. Continue to cook until mixture turns a deep golden brown, about 300°F on a candy thermometer, 5 to 8 minutes. Stir in vanilla and almonds. Remove from heat and immediately scrape out onto an unbuttered baking sheet, using a wooden spoon to spread the mixture flat and separate the nuts as much as possible. Let cool until set, about 20 minutes.

Break apart into chunks or coarsely chop nuts and transfer to an airtight container. Store at room temperature for up to 2 weeks.

1 cup plus 2 table-
spoons sugar

1½ tablespoons light
corn syrup

¼ cup water

½ cup (1 stick)
unsalted butter

⅛ teaspoon salt

1 teaspoon vanilla
extract

3 cups whole almonds
(about 1 pound)

variation
Substitute 3 cups peanuts or macadamia nuts for almonds.

chocolate peanut bark

MAKES ABOUT 4 CUPS Unlike most chocolate nut barks, this candy is more about the peanuts, which are coated with just enough chocolate to hold them together. Leave the bark in larger chunks to eat on its own, or chop it to sprinkle on sundaes, stir into softened vanilla ice cream, or press into the sides of ice cream sandwiches.

Line 2 baking sheets with parchment or waxed paper.

Bring about 2 inches water to a boil in a saucepan or the bottom of a double boiler; remove from heat. Place chocolate in a large heatproof bowl or in the top of double boiler. Set bowl over hot water and let stand, stirring occasionally with a flexible spatula, until melted and smooth, about 15 minutes.

Remove bowl of melted chocolate from pan of hot water and fold in peanuts, turning until nuts are evenly coated. Spread chocolate-coated nuts in a thin layer on baking sheets. Refrigerate or let stand at room temperature until chocolate is firm, 20 to 40 minutes. Remove nuts from baking sheets and break apart into chunks or coarsely chop. Store in an airtight container at room temperature for up to 2 weeks.

8 ounces bittersweet chocolate, finely chopped

3 cups roasted, unsalted peanuts (about 1 pound)

variations

Substitute 3 cups almonds, macadamias, whole espresso beans, or broken waffle-cone pieces (stir gently when coating waffle-cone pieces with the chocolate) for the peanuts.

chocolate whipped cream

MAKES ABOUT 2 CUPS What better way to top off a hot fudge sundae than with this fluffy, cocoa-flavored whipped cream?

1 cup heavy cream

3 tablespoons Dutch-process cocoa powder

3 tablespoons powdered sugar

In a bowl, with an electric mixer on high speed, whip cream until slightly thickened. Sift cocoa powder and powdered sugar over cream and whip gently until cream holds soft peaks. Use immediately, or cover and chill up to 2 hours.

caramel whipped cream

MAKES ABOUT 2 CUPS This rich whipped cream is easy to make and great for topping ice cream sundaes and parfaits.

½ cup caramel sauce (from recipe on page 78 or purchased), at room temperature

1 cup heavy cream

Spoon caramel sauce into a large bowl. In another bowl, with an electric mixer on high speed, whip cream until it holds medium peaks. Stir about one third of the whipped cream into the caramel sauce. Gently fold the remaining whipped cream into the caramel mixture. Whisk gently to thicken, if desired. Use immediately, or cover and chill up to 2 hours.

homemade
ice
creams

Dark Chocolate Ice Cream, page 91

Nothing tastes quite like ice cream you've made yourself. The recipes in this chapter start with a custard base. The key to making a base is to cook the custard mixture gently over low heat, removing it from the heat as soon as it thickens, just enough to coat the back of a spoon. A heatproof flexible spatula is a good tool for stirring the custard as it cooks; scrape the bottom of the pot as you stir.

Straining the hot base through a fine-mesh strainer is not strictly necessary for all of the recipes in this chapter, but I recommend doing so. This step removes any cooked egg from the custard and ensures a homogenous mixture.

Once the custard base has been strained, it must be chilled, preferably overnight, before being frozen in an ice cream maker. The colder the base is, the more quickly it will freeze. This is particularly important if you're using the kind of ice cream maker with a prefrozen cylinder, which generally thaws out within about 20 minutes.

When homemade ice cream comes out of the machine, it will be very soft-set, at which point you may stir in the additions. You can eat it at this stage if you like, but to scoop or to use in most of the recipes in this book, the ice cream will need to be transferred to an airtight container and hardened in the freezer for several hours or overnight.

vanilla bean ice cream

MAKES ABOUT 1 QUART Vanilla beans are expensive, but there is no substitute for the real thing in vanilla ice cream. They contribute tell-tale black specks as well as a flavor and fragrance that are almost floral. Whole vanilla beans are sold in jars in the spice sections of most supermarkets, and in specialty food stores. Choose plump, moist, and shiny vanilla beans. This recipe makes a rich, custard-style ice cream that gets a golden color from the egg yolks.

2½ cups heavy cream
1½ cups whole milk
¾ cup sugar
1 vanilla bean
6 egg yolks

Combine cream, milk, and sugar in a medium heavy-bottomed saucepan. Cut vanilla bean in half lengthwise and use the tip of a small knife to scrape out seeds; add both seeds and pod to pan. Bring to a simmer over medium heat, stirring to dissolve sugar. Remove from heat, cover, and let stand 30 minutes. Return pan to stove and bring the mixture back to a simmer over low heat.

In a bowl, beat egg yolks lightly to blend. Whisk ½ cup of the hot cream mixture into egg yolks; pour yolk mixture back into pan. Stir constantly over low heat until mixture thickens just enough to lightly coat the back of a spoon. Do not let boil.

Pour custard through a fine-mesh strainer into a clean bowl and discard residue. Refrigerate custard or place bowl in an ice bath until cool. Cover bowl with plastic wrap and refrigerate until custard is very cold, at least several hours or up to 1 day.

Freeze the chilled custard in an ice cream maker according to the manufacturer's instructions. Transfer ice cream to an airtight container and freeze at least 6 hours, until firm, or up to 1 week.

strawberry ice cream

MAKES ABOUT 1½ QUARTS   Make this fresh, pink ice cream when strawberries are ripe and plentiful. This recipe incorporates both puréed and chopped strawberries. You can prepare and refrigerate the puréed strawberries the day before you freeze the ice cream, but macerate the roughly chopped strawberries about 20 minutes before you plan to freeze the ice cream.

1⅓ cups heavy cream

⅔ cup whole milk

¾ cup sugar

4 egg yolks

1½ pounds fresh strawberries (three 8-ounce baskets), rinsed and hulled

½ teaspoon vanilla extract

Combine cream, milk, and ½ cup of the sugar in a medium heavy-bottomed saucepan. Bring mixture to a simmer over medium heat, stirring to dissolve sugar. Reduce heat to low.

In a bowl, beat egg yolks lightly to blend. Whisk ½ cup of the hot cream mixture into egg yolks; pour yolk mixture back into pan. Stir constantly over low heat until mixture becomes thick enough to lightly coat the back of a spoon. Do not let boil.

Pour the custard through a fine-mesh strainer into a clean bowl. Refrigerate custard or place bowl in an ice bath until cool. Cover bowl with plastic wrap and refrigerate until custard is very cold, at least several hours or up to 1 day.

Purée 1 pound of the strawberries in a blender or food processor until smooth. Press the purée through a fine-mesh strainer, using a flexible spatula to extract as much juice as possible from the seeds and pulp (you should have about 1⅓ cups purée). Cover and refrigerate purée until you're ready to freeze the ice cream, up to 1 day.

Just before freezing ice cream, rinse and coarsely chop remaining 8 ounces strawberries. Transfer to a small bowl and stir in remaining ¼ cup sugar. Let stand at room temperature for 20 minutes.

Whisk strawberry purée, macerated chopped strawberries, and vanilla into chilled custard until completely incorporated. Freeze the mixture in an ice cream maker according to the manufacturer's instructions. Transfer ice cream to an airtight container and freeze at least 6 hours, until firm, or up to 1 week.

dark chocolate ice cream

MAKES ABOUT 1½ QUARTS   This chocolate ice cream tastes like frozen chocolate mousse, and is possibly the darkest, richest chocolate ice cream you'll ever eat. The chocolate custard base thickens appreciably as it cools, so refrigerate it no longer than about 3 hours before freezing it in an ice cream maker.

Bring about 2 inches water to a boil in a saucepan or the bottom of a double boiler; remove from heat. Combine chocolate and ¼ cup of the cream in a heatproof bowl or in the top of double boiler. Set bowl over hot water and let stand, stirring occasionally with a flexible spatula, until melted and smooth, about 15 minutes.

Combine remaining 2 cups cream and the milk and sugar in a medium heavy-bottomed saucepan. Bring mixture to a simmer over medium heat, stirring to dissolve sugar. Reduce heat to low.

In a bowl, beat egg yolks lightly to blend. Whisk ½ cup of the hot cream mixture into egg yolks; pour yolk mixture back into saucepan. Stir constantly over low heat until mixture thickens just enough to lightly coat the back of a spoon. Do not let boil.

Remove from heat and whisk the melted chocolate mixture into the hot custard until well blended.

Pour the chocolate custard through a fine-mesh strainer into a clean bowl and discard residue. Refrigerate custard or place bowl in an ice bath until cool. Cover bowl with plastic wrap and refrigerate until custard is very cold and thickened to about the consistency of chocolate pudding, 2 to 3 hours.

Stir vanilla into chilled custard. Freeze in an ice cream maker according to the manufacturer's instructions. Transfer ice cream to an airtight container and freeze at least 6 hours, until firm, or up to 1 week.

8 ounces bittersweet chocolate, very finely chopped

2¼ cups heavy cream

1½ cups whole milk

⅔ cup sugar

6 egg yolks

2 teaspoons vanilla extract

coffee bean ice cream

MAKES ABOUT 1 QUART The more finely you chop the coffee beans, the stronger the flavor of the finished ice cream. If you prefer a mild coffee flavor, chop the beans coarsely.

2½ cups heavy cream

1½ cups whole milk

¾ cup sugar

1 cup dark-roasted coffee beans, finely chopped

6 egg yolks

2 teaspoons vanilla extract

Combine cream, milk, sugar, and coffee beans in a medium heavy-bottomed saucepan. Bring mixture just to a simmer over medium heat, stirring to dissolve sugar. Remove from heat, cover, and let stand 1 hour. Pour mixture through a fine strainer into a bowl; discard coffee beans. Rinse or wipe out any coffee bean residue in the saucepan. Return the strained cream mixture to the saucepan and bring to a simmer over low heat.

In a bowl, beat egg yolks lightly to blend. Whisk ½ cup of the hot cream mixture into egg yolks; pour yolk mixture back into pan. Stir constantly over low heat until mixture thickens just enough to lightly coat the back of a spoon. Do not let boil.

Pour custard through a fine-mesh strainer into a clean bowl and discard residue. Refrigerate custard or place bowl in an ice bath until cool. Cover bowl with plastic wrap and refrigerate until custard is very cold, at least several hours or up to 1 day.

Stir vanilla into the chilled custard and freeze in an ice cream maker according to the manufacturer's instructions. Transfer ice cream to an airtight container and freeze at least 6 hours, until firm, or up to 1 week.

index

table of equivalents

The exact equivalents in the following tables have been rounded for convenience.

liquid/dry measures

U.S.	METRIC
¼ teaspoon	1.25 milliliters
½ teaspoon	2.5 milliliters
1 teaspoon	5 milliliters
1 tablespoon (3 teaspoons)	15 milliliters
1 fluid ounce (2 tablespoons)	30 milliliters
¼ cup	60 milliliters
⅓ cup	80 milliliters
½ cup	120 milliliters
1 cup	240 milliliters
1 pint (2 cups)	480 milliliters
1 quart (4 cups, 32 ounces)	960 milliliters
1 gallon (4 quarts)	3.84 liters
1 ounce (by weight)	28 grams
1 pound	454 grams
2.2 pounds	1 kilogram

length

U.S.	METRIC
⅛ inch	3 millimeters
¼ inch	6 millimeters
½ inch	12 millimeters
1 inch	2.5 centimeters

oven temperature

FAHRENHEIT	CELSIUS	GAS
250	120	½
275	140	1
300	150	2
325	160	3
350	180	4
375	190	5
400	200	6
425	220	7
450	230	8
475	240	9
500	260	10